Death Obscura

Poems

RICK BURSKY

Sarabande Books

LOUISVILLE, KENTUCKY

Managing Editor
Sarabande Books, Inc.
2234 Dundee Road, Suite 200
Louisville, KY 40205

Library of Congress Cataloging-in-Publication Data

Bursky, Rick.
  Death obscura : poems / Rick Bursky. — 1st ed.
      p. cm.
  ISBN 978-1-932511-87-1 (pbk. : alk. paper)
  I. Title.
  PS3602.U774D43 2010
  811'.6—dc22

                                    2010004649

Cover design by Robin Evens.
Interior text design by Kirkby Gann Tittle.
Manufactured in Canada.
This book is printed on acid-free paper.

Sarabande Books is a nonprofit literary organization.

This project is supported in part by an award from the
National Endowment for the Arts.

The Kentucky Arts Council, the state arts agency,
supports Sarabande Books with state tax dollars and
federal funding from the National Endowment for the
Arts.

for Alexis Orgera

CONTENTS

ACKNOWLEDGMENTS

The author is grateful to the following journals where the poems have previously appeared, sometimes in a different form.

Field; *Iowa Review*; *Hotel Amerika*; *Agni Online*; *The New Ohio Review*; *New CollAge Magazine*; *88*; *Epoch*; *Whiskey Island Magazine*; *West Branch*; *Swink Magazine*; *Midwest Quarterly*; *The Dirty Goat*; *The Tampa Review*; *The Saint Ann's Review*; and in the chapbook *The Invention of Fiction*, published by Hollyridge Press.

For encouragement, friendship and careful reading of many of these poems, the author owes a debt of gratitude to Larry Gorlick, Ian Randall Wilson, Nin Andrews, George Higgins, Elayne Boosler, Bill Siddons, Patty Smith, Arthur and Ellen Behar, Laura Kasischke, Deborah Beville, Heather McElhatton, Anne Gallagher, Sarah Cathcart, Sariah Dorbin, Richard Garcia, Peter Serchuk, Patty Smith, Maryam Mohseni, Lori Davis, Antoinette de Paiva, Robin and Erik Evens, Patrick and Mary Ballogg, Harold and Rebecca Watson, Sarah Gorham, Jeffrey Skinner, Jane Hirshfield, Mark and Melanie Monteiro, Shari Becker, Tony Caggiano, Bruce and Nancy Silverman, Helene Cote; Helen Bursky and my brother, Alan Bursky.

Death Obscura

The Mandolin

This was the night police chased the musicians from the roof.
Yes, the building was abandoned, waiting for the steel ball
to swing from a chain and smash walls.
But the old women across the street couldn't sleep.
This was the night someone hid a mandolin in a garbage can,
just below a filthy sweater, as if they expected someone
to lift the lid and look. This was the night
the pay phone on the corner continued to ring.
The night the sky remained dark longer than it had a right to.
And the dust that would rise into that sky, just waiting.

Then What

Four years after burying the cat she decided to dig its remains.
The gardening spade used to plant flowers along the porch,
she would dig with that. Surely the skeleton would tell her
something, but if it didn't, then what? When she pushed
the spade into the ground the moon was low
over her shoulder. Once below the tough roots
of the grass, the earth was soft. She dug through them with her
    hands.
Isn't it enough to be curious? That would be the answer if
    questioned,
though she didn't plan to share this with many.
And behind her on the clothesline, a blouse and the white
    underwear
she meant to retrieve earlier but was distracted by a phone call.
She remembered the grave deeper, but in minutes
touched something brittle and curved. The underwear billowed
in a breeze that grew into a gust and glowed over her and the
    grave.

The Virtu

This wasn't the first time I'd watched a woman
wear high heels in the shower.
Closed-toe this time. Her toes weren't painted
and she didn't want anyone to see.
After she told me this, her head tilted back.
Water masked her face in a way
not possible if she still had been turned
to me as I stood at the sink shaving,
then brushing my teeth.
An inconsequential detail,
whether or not she was watching,
Water darkened the red shoes.
The damaged world spun beneath.
Her balance, of course, was perfect.

Lament for the Persians

I named seven stars after her left eye.
Astronomers protested.
Dictators where jealous.
Two religious leaders were outraged.
But I wouldn't budge.
So the heavenly mapmakers
checked the spelling and went to work.
Seventeen months later, a complaint
from an archaeology professor at the University of Cairo.
In 471 BC Xerxes, King of Persia,
named those same seven stars
after the left eye of his mother, Queen Atosa
—that's what his letter said. It came with a photograph
of the inscription on her coffin.
What led him to believe I read Persian I'll never know.
Though one night in the desert I struggled
through a sentence in that language.
My tongue could never find
the sound for that vocabulary.
The world might continue to collect catastrophe
—something I was sure the complaining
archaeology professor would agree with
—but the deep beauty of her left eye

would continue until those seven stars exploded,

which for practical purposes is forever.

If it was the right eye, instead of the left,

that I'd stared at when she turned to order tequila

those seven stars would still belong to Queen Atosa.

The Aerodynamics

The night she walked to the house
she held a string; on the other end,
fifty-three feet in the air, a kite.
Wind provided the aerodynamics.
Does every collaboration
need to be explained?
She tied the string to the mailbox
left the kite to float until morning.
Every night this happens.
She sleeps, I listen, darkness
slides through us both.

The next morning
the string still curved into the sky
but the kite was gone.
This was the morning
newspapers announced
the *Mona Lisa* was stolen.
This was the morning
it snowed in Los Angeles,
the morning I wore gloves
to pull from the sky
fifty-three feet of frozen string.

Heroine in Repose

I wasn't sure if she kissed me
or simply used her lips
to push my face away. Yes,
the moist warmth was enjoyable,
but when my head was forced
back over the top of the sofa
the intention grayed.

Earlier that day I planned
to quit my job and pursue
a career writing romantic novels
that would be confused as memoirs.
But if I couldn't distinguish
between a kiss and a push
what chance do I have
of writing romantic novels
that would be confused as memoirs?

After the kiss, and I prefer
to think it was a kiss,
she sank back into the pillows
and watched me
out of the corner of her eye.

The Chrysalis

"If you were me, would you love you?"
Though I had more information than the caterpillar
when asked if it wants to become a butterfly,
I remained silent. Could feel her question in my chest.
We were at a Chinese restaurant.
I leaned in to kiss her. She leaned back and asked.
The next day at work, concentrating
on my responsibilities, the accuracy
of foot-long wooden rulers, became difficult.

"If you were me, would you love you?"
Whether or not she was the first woman
to ask me that question is unimportant.
Don't be so quick to believe
that caterpillars want to be butterflies.
To be honest, I was afraid. In the chrysalis,
organs and other structures disassemble,
then remodel. Sometimes this lasts the winter.
She took the little plastic sword in her fingers,
lifted the olive from the martini,
put it between her teeth, held it there, grinned
as if to say "well." Why do women do this?

Two Sonnets for the Left Ventricle of the Heart

for Anne

One

She's in my arms, crying, about what is none of your business,
Nor the business of this poem. This poem is about the way I
  embrace
Anguish, hold it like a bag of light bulbs—this is about
  tenderness.
No, that's not entirely true. Think of broken glass, I'll make a
  case
For her in my arms later. How dark is a life at night? Curtains
  drawn,
Blankets pulled to just below the nose, eyes closed, other
Than socks and shoes there's nothing to count on.
So why bother getting out of bed in the morning? Her lover
Knows a bag of groceries doesn't replace the rhythm or sound
Of a tongue. Her crying is an exclamation point, a pat on the
  back,
Something gone right that can't be undone; a wave that found
A reason to fall on the shore and is no longer frozen in its
  tracks.
This can't go on for much longer. Gravity pulls on the
  distressed
With as much spite as it pulls at a man falling or a woman's
  breasts.

11

Two

There are two sides to each closed door, each half-moon, each
 life.

I've been a borrower, took shoes, shirt, money for gas and a hat.

The list can go on; there's lots missing. Still, I'm not borrowing
 a wife

Just for the sake of a rhyme or dramatic tension. Besides, that

Would cheapen the poem, not to mention what it would do to
 me.

That's where she comes in, weather in progress looking for a
 place

To put the customary beautiful day-after; even the stormiest
 sea

Tires of raging at the sky. So, which of us is the sea? the sky?
 Whose face

Is lined with more terrifying clouds? She doesn't care anymore.

There's salt in the salt shaker, pepper in the pepper shaker,
 milk and eggs

In the refrigerator. A kitchen, someone once wrote, is a
 metaphor

For something or another, I don't remember what. I know, it
 begs

For an explanation but I don't have one. It just feels good here,
The way a full moon feels in a night sky, anything else is just
    fear.

Sutra

A porch once screened-in
now broken as the house it clings to;
thirteen years abandoned,
a punctuation mark
that gathers dark fog
between trees in the Uwharrie Forest.
I never told what happened
or who we met,
me and Doug Holderfield,
our knives unsheathed dragging us
to the noise in the grass,
afraid to turn back.
To insure silence
we lifted our boots
clear of the foliage
before moving forward.
There's no one to praise
if your prayer isn't answered.
The next morning not a word
was said about the night
as we marched back to our barracks.

The Scratch

for Harry Watson

Our fingers ignored the cold rain
that dripped from the knuckles
as the bipod locked into place.
The steel tube leaned into the angle.
A poncho was stretched across
the mud, four rocket-shaped mortars
on top, and on top of them another poncho.
Someone whispered into a radio.
Someone pulled the propellant
from a mortar like strips of cheese.
Someone cranked to traverse.
Someone would hurt
their eye, picking something up
when kneeling to stare
through that small glass sight
at the black and white aiming stakes.
Two thousand meters away
no one was expecting the sky to explode.
Two days away, steam rising
from creamed beef in large tin cans.
All forgotten until twenty-three years
later, an ophthalmologist in Texarkana
comments on a scratch on a cornea.

Cardiology

Seven years ago I bought a pair of crutches,
just in case. Each Sunday morning I practiced
walking with them, bent my left leg back
from the knee as if the ankle had been mangled
while stepping onto an escalator.
I also practiced with the other leg unable
to support its proper share of weight.
A surgeon sold hearts he carved from oak.
Some people have nothing to lose,
he said, sanding a pulmonary vein.
I cooked breakfast with an arm in a sling
made from an ill-fitting shirt. Yes, practice.
Once the beauty of the oak is absolute
the surgeon places it where a heart is required,
then sews with attention not typically lavished
on those who've lost everything.
Twice each week the phone rings
at three in the morning. I never answer.
Someone is practicing sad news, I'm certain.
An oak will one day grow from my heart.
No amount of practice can prepare you
for the first push through dirt.

The Study

I followed her across the dance floor,
down the dark hallway and behind
the defective pay phone that rang if slapped
with the palm of your hand. I tasted her nipples
through the thin silk bra.
One tasted like aluminum, the other ash.

Then she asked for a dollar.
She only said "oops" when she let
her empty martini glass fall.
She was the first person to tell me
The Last of the Mohicans was Stalin's favorite book,
and sometimes he even dressed like an Indian.

I'm not drunk, she said, I'm a science
waiting to be studied, a name that needs
to be added to The Periodic Table of Elements
between iron and dust. Her fingernails,
she thought of them as rusted iron.
Dust was her favorite element.

The odor of urine from a doorless bathroom.
The chronic concussion of music

shook the black plasterboard walls.

The purpose of this story waiting

to be scraped from the tip of her tongue.

Of course, we never talked about this at the office.

The Surface of the Tongue

When I stuck my tongue into the light socket
a faint glow pulsed from under my fingernails,
and my eyeballs, oh, my eyeballs were so white.
I thought to study my teeth to see if in that shocking instant
they brightened. But imagine the difficulty
of holding a mirror close to the mouth
while standing close to the wall, tongue in a light socket.
I was thinking of ways to impress her.
Upon realizing that few men had done this before
I immediately began to practice.

While standing with my tongue in the light socket
I made a mental list of things to tell her.
I've dedicated myself to calm, is first.
I've convinced myself to miracle, is second.
To avoid depression I've taught myself to sob while asleep
—I'm undecided about that one.
Humans are inherently electrical.
It's what separates us from the dead.
The shock required to start or stop
a heart is meaningless desperation.

While standing with my tongue in the light socket

I discovered a rip in my heart,

the septum ventricle to be exact,

allowing the deoxygenated blood in the left ventricle

to drown the oxygenated blood in the right ventricle.

Romance requires collaboration.

Collaboration requires incentive.

I felt the surface of my tongue begin to burn,

that was my first taste of the incentive.

The Argonaut Years

for Alicia

I

She dreamed she pulled her face from my lips
and they tore off, clung to her cheek
like leeches which she immediately ripped from her face.
Embarrassed by the unintended meanness
of the gesture she put them in the palm of my hand
to have them sewn back at a later time.
As she told me about the dream
I finished brushing my teeth, spit the last
of the toothpaste and water into the sink.
I was an argonaut in her life, but didn't mind,
love makes explorers of us all.
The neighbor's cat left gifts at her door.
On the sidewalk, a broken piano
abandoned three days. A man
walking by stopped to play.
When does the decay set in?

II

This is when the decay sets in.
I wiped the toothpaste from my face
and kissed her but she pulled her face from my lips
and they tore off, clung to her cheek

like leeches which she immediately ripped from her face.
Embarrassed by the unintended meanness
of the gesture she put them in the palm of my hand
to have them sewn back at a later time.
I held a towel to my bloody face,
wrapped the lips in napkins.
It will be years before she forgives me,
years more before I learn what for.
She returned to bed, sat upright,
her knees pulled to her chest.
Her hands, she waited
until I was gone before washing.

Judas

I bought a nine-year-old pickup truck
for the convenience of Judas,
the one-hundred-year-old tortoise
she gave me when she left.
Two or three times a week,
I took Judas to the ocean.
He rode in a plastic wading pool
filled with water that I secured in the bed.
Awkward and slow on land,
his four hundred pounds curved
through the swollen ocean's clouds graceful
as a ballerina in an old Dutch painting.
The red that blossoms from hands
when you nail a man to water is a map.
I held the sides of his shell, followed like a cape
through schools of silver fish, through
the thermocline's floor, through dark patches
where whatever sinks sinks faster.
Deep in the ocean it rains, Judas showed me.
Deep in the ocean nurses sleep in salt-crusted caves,
Judas showed me. I held breath
in the balloon of my mouth.
This is where I first thought sacrifice.

I was a shoebox filled with the past,
Judas showed me this, too.
Notice how briefly she was in this narrative.
Ascending, air expands in the lungs.
Ascending, a survival principle.
This, of course, is a theory. Other theories
include providence and literature.
Squeeze a beating heart tight as you can
and you'll fall asleep;
for this there is no explanation.

You Can Talk to a Ghost All You Want, It Won't Change a Thing

for Alicia

I left my shoes in the buffalo grass, ran barefoot
with a butterfly net catching gods.
And what will a god think
stuffed in a matchbox, gift-wrapped
on the kitchen table beside toast and tea
waiting for her, not yet fully awake,
one eye open, and not yet the other;
and while one leg finds its way from under
the blanket and is groping for a slipper, not yet the other.

Can you smell the ocean? Did you shake the sand
from your hair, comb away the salt?
Last night, the cockroaches rebelled,
you thought it was a dream we shared.
Last night, when you put your ear
in my mouth what were you listening for?
Last night, you demonstrated it was science,
not love. Though I might have that reversed
—that's the trouble with love.

The Silences

for Deborah

She didn't speak for twenty-four hours.
This was the first silence she insisted on.
Everything she needed to say was stored
in the cupboard with the thin-lipped
wine glasses that we never used.
Though I don't remember if she did
actually need to say anything.
The second silence was mine,
not a word for twenty-four hours.
I should have mentioned it earlier, this was her idea.
I should also mention this wasn't meant to suggest
that she was tired of my voice,
at least this was the last thing she said
before saying nothing. I tossed everything
I needed to say in the corner of the bedroom
with the dirty laundry. And like the dirty laundry
it was soon cleaned. The third silence,
this silence, we shared. Remember,
this was her idea, not mine.
Mine was to sing to each other during sex.
Didn't even have to be the same song.
I was planning on Italian folk songs.

Early rock and roll would have been her choice,

something by her favorite, The Del-Vikings.

The first time I disrobed her

she sang, "who am I, the voodoo man;

who am I, the voodoo man." Thus my guess

on what she would have sung.

But she preferred silence.

The Decorum

A bouquet of radishes,
that was her favorite gift.
The cool bitterness that filled
the mouth when her teeth split
the small, red fists.
The kitten someone gave her
drowned in the toilet.
How do you explain that?
Someone once asked if she missed
how it rubbed against her leg
and purred as she spooned food
into a small metal dish.
Someone once asked her
if she missed the way her husband read
to her each night. Seven years ago
she left him, no explanation.
How do you explain that?
She quartered the radishes,
mixed them in yogurt for breakfast.
Sometimes shared them
with the kitten and husband.

The Immortals

In the painting of the young couple kissing
on a bench in a museum hallway
I'm the subject of the portrait
hanging on the wall behind them.
I'm wearing the blue velvet jacket
of an eighteenth-century Prussian cavalry officer
standing beside a white horse that's too large to be accurate.
Though I'm rendered with lifelike precision. Obviously,
I couldn't have served in the eighteenth-century Prussian
    cavalry.
I don't speak German, and was born centuries late.
I'm not the first person to pay
a famous artist to be in a painting.
Though I wanted to be the man being kissed.
Unfortunately, my famous artist didn't believe
a girl that lovely would kiss me in public.
I offered photographs of previous lovers
but unless one was kissing me on a bench
in a museum hallway his answer was no.
That's unfair. Otherwise I'm pleased
with the painting. The couple kissing,
I suspect, also paid to be in the painting.
Though I'm certain they were strangers.

Her eyes are open, peering at where
we might stand admiring the painting.

Instead of resting on his cheek, the palm of her hand
is pushing proving that while she desired
to live forever in art her desire didn't include him.
I once fell thirty-seven feet
from a railroad bridge into a river.
Riding the ambulance to the hospital
is when I decided to pay a famous artist
to put me in a painting.
What brought the woman to the painting
is something I've often fantasized about.
The oxygen mask's elastic strap
pinched the back of my neck.
I kept the discomfort to myself.

The Separation

My father built a wall in the middle of the yard;
five feet high and seven feet long,
separating nothing there from nothing not there.
At night he whispered to the wall.
Mother said, "What a man whispers
in the shadow of his wall is his business alone."
Large flat stones, mortar, moonlight,
the damp quiet—father leaned against the wall
like a man waiting in an alley.

After he died mother closed her eyes
and placed her ear against the wall.
One side of the wall was love.
One side of the wall was longing.
Later she donated the wall to a church.
One side of the wall became sky.
One side of the wall became earth.
Mother never said what she heard
or if she heard anything at all.

Ocular Triptych

He once feared he would swallow it,
or blind it drinking coffee,
but the man with a third eye in his tongue
learned to think of the eyelid like the door
of a vault protecting a terrible secret,
or perhaps a trapdoor to a flooded basement
where old music boxes
and a pair of crutches float.

The man with a third eye in his tongue
could see his breath shaped
into words by the mouth's warm walls.
At night, he closed the eyes in his head
and opened his mouth. His third eye
blinked, caught the black snapshots
of dreams as he slept.
His mother told a doctor,
don't talk to me about mistakes.

The Strangers

Three men stood on the edge of a grave.
The coffin's polished lid reflected the sky.
One of the men wanted to toss a cigarette
into the grave, you could tell
by the way he held the cigarette
and sucked smoke into his mouth.
The third man wore the nicest suit,
fresh creases and black as the night sky
without the monotony of stars.
The grave, nothing more than a vomitorium.
The shined shoes, nothing more than temporary.
The second man did and said nothing
of note. He was me. The gravedigger
climbed into the tractor, pulled the lever
to lower the shovel and it started to rain.

The History of Traitors

Every army has one. The night before battle
Caesar's cousin dulled the edges of swords.
Later, the cousin's severed head
—a black ball of maggots and flies—
on the side of the road.
No mention of what to do with this information.
God is the original traitor.
Ask the defeated facing the firing squad.
Hesitation is an indictment. Late in the Cold War,
the United States Army coated spoons
with a chemical that turned orange under ultraviolet light
once exposed to an enzyme produced by stress.
The theory was that it would be present in traitors.
It is said that seventy-two
of these spoons were placed
in army mess halls in Korea.
An army counterintelligence manual observes
that traitors smile more than other soldiers.

The Meaning of Numbers

The Threes

Again, the coughing woke him.
Each heave shook the bed, the floor, the room.
This is how the three mornings began.
Again, he stared from the open window at the still
and dark street. Three times it stared back.
He massaged his neck, a gesture proving
he confused the outside with the in.

Before sunrise, wearing only underwear
he sat on the porch and sipped tea with milk.
The three shoes he wanted to throw away
remained beside the door for at least one more week.

The Fives

On the floor below the basement stairs,
five tobacco cans filled with old nails
from abandoned houses. Each nail pulled
carefully as not to bend and if it did, straightened
with five quick blows of an old hammer
—metal talking to metal, questions
and promises taking turns and lies.

Without nails a house collapses in about five minutes,
but it takes five years for the sky to fill the space.

The Sevens

In the attic, skeletons of hornets filled a cardboard box
and on the table the shovel
with which someone planned to dig their grave.
How long had it been since that plan was abandoned?
Dust takes seven years to blanket
a windowless room. Seven years
and not even the sound of the moon.

In the café below, a woman in a black dress
played solitaire every day for seven years.
In a bowl on her table, seven fresh roses.
The aroma remained even if she lost.

The Curator of Closets

I bought my first empty closet on a warm spring day at an
art fair in Vicenza, Italy. Girls rolled up their pants. Their
legs could support marble tables in museums. Close the door
and you'd swear you heard a bee sting. I stood in my second
empty closet for hours. It was narrow, my nose prevented
the door from closing. Sometimes I believe those hours were
my happiest. They said a crocodile was killed in my third
empty closet. The only evidence was the stench, similar to
the smell of overripe watermelon. My fourth empty closet was
the color of someone leaving. The back wall was shellacked,
glossy enough to shave, something I did with the assistance
of a flashlight. Each time I looked inside the fifth I was afraid.
A voice said, "What time is it, what time is it." Yes, said it
twice, then the empty silence that I love. Once something
becomes unimportant it's abandoned in an empty closet. An
elephant falls at the same speed as a pebble. Think about that,
an elephant falls at the same speed as a pebble. Imagine finding
that written at the bottom of an empty closet—even the laws
of physics can't maintain their importance in the closets we're
discussing.

Death Obscura

1. The Concern

Tomorrow at three twenty-one I will die. I don't know how.
But I know it will happen. Thirteen years ago I gave a woman
sixty-five dollars to tell me what will happen to me. I knew
the basics. My hair will gray, I'll gain weight; and like you, will
find myself suspicious of those days when a deep orange sun
shines, the wind blows from too many directions and while
everyone seems polite there's a treacherous silence about. For
sixty-five dollars I expected to learn other things. We sat in her
kitchen in Port Jefferson Station, a suburb of New York. She
had short gray hair and an accent I couldn't name. On the wall
was a trite expression embroidered on cloth, "God bless our
happy home." She offered me tea. She said in twenty-two days
I would lose my job. It took twenty-three. She said a woman
from Ohio would love me for five months. And a woman from
Ohio did love me, but for seven months. All close enough. The
other day I fell asleep on the sofa and dreamed I was back in
that kitchen. If not for that dream I would have completely
forgotten about tomorrow. I want to believe that the past is
not a messenger for the future, perhaps a metaphor, but no
messenger. Under my bed there's a .45 caliber semi-automatic
pistol, a P220 Sig Sauer, to be exact; in the kitchen, at least two

dozen knives of various sizes. I'm curious about what role they might play in the coming events.

2. Without Explanation

Ayano Kobayashi, a forty-two-year-old bookkeeper for a shoe manufacturer in Northern Japan, sat next to her cousin on a bus. The cousin thought Ayano fell asleep. At the same moment the cousin realized something was very wrong, the bus stopped in front of Nagoya University Hospital. I was once ordered into a river at night to retrieve a body. Do both eyes close together or does one lag with cowardliness? Ayano was pronounced dead in the emergency room. A clean white sheet placed over the body. Her shoes removed and given to the cousin. The body moved to the hospital morgue in the basement where it was examined and x-rayed. The date was August 4th, 1973. I am one of the few people who believe that the unseasonable rain had something to do with what happened. Eventually, the electricity in every brain stops, leaving it dark as a night sky after a lightning storm. And then what? Seventeen hours after Ayano Kobayashi was pronounced dead, she was found walking barefoot and sobbing through a basement hallway. It doesn't matter how the doctors explained this. Three weeks later Ayano drowned herself in a public swimming pool at night. Her neatly folded clothes were found on a nearby bench. There was no note, no history of depression.

3. The Obituaries

In 1900, seventy-two colleges offered courses in writing obituaries. I wonder, though not often, if this was out of respect for death or life. Three colleges have closed since then. A well-crafted obituary has undertones of a self-effacing apology. By 1965, only four courses remained. Three ended in 1973, and the last was dropped in 1977. Though people have continued to die. Antoinette De Paiva was an associate professor at Brooklyn College when she taught the last course. When I interviewed Ms. De Paiva over the phone she was retired in Lancaster, California. A polite woman, she asked if I would mind if she ate midget plums picked from a tree in her yard and smoked Pall Malls as we spoke. There were pauses in the conversation when she drew on the cigarettes, followed by quick bursts of facts, as if to make up for the silence. She had rewritten her own obituary one hundred and eleven times, "like a self-portrait," and offered to write a draft of mine. I told her my age and said I was too young. She said I wasn't.

4. Of Resignation

In 1938 the University of California at San Francisco turned
down an offer of three and a half million dollars to fund
research that would answer the question of life after death.
The anonymous donor then offered the gift to Leland Stanford
Jr. University, where it was accepted. The project was called
the Wilson Funded Study. Most likely, the name Wilson was a
pseudonym. We don't know if it was suffering or joy that led to
the gift. All too often, conclusions share the odor of promises.
But Stanford agreed. Whatever was concluded was forgotten
in a locked file cabinet in the basement of Encina Hall. When
the building was renovated it was decided to dispose of the
file cabinet unopened. Only moments before the cabinet was
hauled away, Sarah Cathcart, an undergraduate on a work/
study scholarship forced the lock. All that remained of the
Wilson Funded Study was held a large green envelope with a
clasp. Inside the envelope were a receipt for nine rolls of film
and two gallons of white paint, dated July 3, 1940, and a blank
sheet of personal stationery belonging to Professor Richard P.
Gabriel. Did the professor intend to take portraits of the dead?
The only information I found connecting him to the project
was a letter of resignation, dated April 16, 1942. He wrote,
". . . the study has forced me to examine my mortality and I

have found little difference between wind pushing rain through
an open window and myself." In the war years that followed
he designed proximity fuses for the navy. In his obituary
the last paragraph said, ". . . enjoyed working late in his den
overlooking a small strand of trees. As a distraction at night he
would sometimes sketch the trees and the shadows between
them, an excuse, he said, to stare into that narrow darkness."

5. The Beautiful Thing

In the Berici Hills above the Northern Italian city of Vicenza it was discovered that there was no educational value in horror films when, at two twenty-three in the morning, an American soldier was swarmed by what he believed were dozens of vampire bats. In the official reports of both the Arma dei Carabinieri and the U.S. Army military police the soldier twice used his portable radio to call for help, calls that were ignored, before moving the selector switch on his M-16 to automatic and firing a magazine of twenty-nine bullets in four seconds at the bats. A solider should know more about death than what he learns in the movies. The bat's razor-sharp upper incisor teeth make a 7 millimeter long and 8 millimeter deep cut into a victim's vein. The bat's saliva has several ingredients that prolong bleeding. One is an anticoagulant that prevents clotting. A second keeps red blood cells from sticking together. A third prevents the vein from constricting near the wound. The soldier, of course, knew nothing of these facts. The beautiful thing about fear is its lack of questions, its obedience to action. None of the thirty-one responding police officers believed it was necessary to recover the spent shell casings. None asked the soldier if he believed the folklore repercussions of being bitten. None of the vampire bats were killed.

6. The Uncomfortable History

My father returned to tell me something important, something
he learned traveling that great distance without his family. We
sat in a diner at night. Steam drifted from untouched coffee
cups in front of us. Headlights from a passing car illuminated
his face. I saw the toll those nineteen years in the grave had
taken. The jaw muscles were tight as tangled roots. Across
the nose the flesh was thin, if there at all. But when he spoke
the voice was his as much as on that day, a month before
death, when he noticed the tape recorder and asked, "Are you
afraid you're going to forget my voice?" I told the therapist
I was troubled, I needed to own something and if I couldn't
own those words, well, yes, I was afraid. "Forgetting dreams
is a survival mechanism triggered in the same corner of the
brain that forces a man struggling on the ocean to take the
final swallow of air" (Doctor Brithe Ingebritsen, University of
Bergen, 1993). The difference between dreaming that a person
returns from the dead and a person actually doing so is the
difference between a tree knocked to the ground by an axe or
by lightning.

The Hypnology

I

A man sits on a bus bench and flips a coin.

It's just after midnight.

The next bus won't arrive for hours.

To keep the cold air off his throat

he buttons his shirt to the top.

He runs his hand over his wrinkled pants leg

like a blind man smoothing

a crumpled note to read the Braille.

This has nothing to do with a bus.

The streetlights are lost planets;

flies are moons.

Heads, return home.

Tails, remain at the bus bench.

The traffic signal clicks three time before changing.

Once, he got into bed without

even removing his shoes.

II

A soft blue light sweeps the kitchen

from a television beside a sink

filled with soapy water.

On the television, two women are riding a train.
After three hours of not being able to sleep
she washes dishes, glasses, and two days' silverware.
She imagines the two women on the television
can see her t-shirt and underwear.
The television is mute;
she doesn't want to hear what they say about her.
A siren in the distance.
An opossum in the shadow of a garbage can.
The dishes are clean.

III

A man sits on the curb smoking a cigarette
while she sleeps; raspy inhales, long exhales,
a forefinger against a thumb
when he flicks a butt into the street
before pulling another from the emptying pack.
She wakes to walk the dog
when the moon is between
a streetlight and a tree.
Her white robe billows in the breeze,

collapses, glows in the chill.
The dog sniffs at the man
in his smoky gray cloud.

There is so little to say.
Isn't this the best use of night,
to make us afraid, make us uncomfortable,
make us stare at the ceiling until morning.
Is sleep a skill or a prize?

IV
Now let me address you, reading
in your car, only lifting your head
when you hear the front door open
and see her coax the dog along the driveway.
Are you embarrassed like the man who can't explain
his presence in a neighbor's dream?

The Original Purpose of the Box

In the Museum of Antiquities,
a guard in a gray uniform stands against the wall.
Once, he heard a woman say, "I don't believe."
Once, he saw a child grow frightened.
Once, the guard told a man with an old camera
on his shoulder that photographs weren't allowed.
Invention is a series of tragedies.
The original purpose of the box
was to contain the emptiness.
Though scholars once thought
it was invented as a place to hide

a length of silk, dagger
or a crucifix from a borrowed god.
In the middle of the room
is where the first box sits.
Tragedy is a series of inventions.
Each wall, the nuance of a different disgrace.
The floor, camel tongues stitched together.
The ceiling changed with the weather.
At night the guard takes the box home.
As he rides the bus it sits on his lap
as if it held his lunch or a gift.

The Waiting

Standing in front of the toilet urinating,
I lowered my head and my glasses fell
into the yellowed water. So much for beauty.
There are parts of ourselves we don't want to touch,
stories told in small gestures.
Using the tips of two fingers I fished them out,
let them soak in a sink of cold water.
That was over a year ago.
The past smells like a lost dog.
The past is so damned tired,
following us around.
The past can be forgotten
for a while, like you can forget
you're wearing glasses.

Sometimes I feel like the man
with an electric tongue,
light bulb glowing in his mouth.
Sometimes I'm afraid
I want to tear out my liver and eat it.
Sometimes I think I smell urine on my glasses.
Salt rises from the ocean,
thick silver clouds that scrape the sky.

I make stories out of mistakes,

it's how I practice forgiveness.

The story about the man who caught a Bengal tiger

with a butterfly net is inspiring.

It doesn't matter if it's true.

The Ritual

A woman sits on the lip of a bathtub
and shaves her legs. A thin red line
on the side of her calf blossoms
in the water at the ankle. On the other side
of the open window, the flicker
of a dying streetlamp, its constant dull buzz
a chorus of blind bees. For now,
her wrinkled blouse
is caught in the light.
The secret of grief is the way it gathers
in the corner of a room,
fits of dust brooms never catch.
She shaves one leg, then the other.

December

When I was a small boy the mural on my bedroom ceiling
was of a steamship bullying its way through a gray ocean. The
prow pushing at the water, and the water roiling, salt-white
like saliva at a baby's lips. The ship's name was painted in
blocky black letters on the bow, S.S. Coffin. I always believed
the artist intended it to be December. I always believed after
the ship passed it would begin to snow. But the Coffin never
passed. It hung there, above, for the rest of my life as the snow
pilled in the attic and turned to ice.

Elegy Written in Four Seasons

Winter

The original color was white, it required no adjectives,
and was easy to see a spider walk across.
A boy with new earmuffs is first
to walk across the snow-covered field
writing his name in the snow
with the yardstick from behind the basement door.
Someday the sky will tire of being black and blue
and bags of seed will be dragged from the shed.
Winter, the ghost of every season,
when everyone pretends
"coffin" is not another word for cradle.

Spring

In the early morning, windows wide
to the luscious odor of winter's corpse,
she sat on the bed painting her toenails,
sheets careless across her thighs,
comfortable in the season of her nakedness,
the season of anything possible.
It was probably a Sunday
and if it wasn't it should have been.

Sun darkens the flesh,
sweat sweetens it.
Later, she'll blame herself,
should have caught the faint odor
of a woman beginning to bury herself
long before her death.
Only spring makes a history
out of a woman painting
her toenails, a history
out of foreign music playing on a radio,
a man in the kitchen
squeezing oranges for juice.

Summer
The premise is simple, a matter of up and down,
give and take, perhaps breaking versus repair.
The little girl flicked her wrist.
The yo-yo plunged, a sharp fall
followed by the undoing
of gravity as it climbed back up the string.
She once asked her father to time the toy,

from plummet to return, one alligator, two alligator.
So there went the summer, warmth fading into coolness,
the speed of alligators barely brushed the buffalo grass
before being jerked back to the beginning.
The neighbor's old collie snapped at fireflies
who in their spectacular instant saw the scratch of
lightning, which to a firefly is God.
The climax of memory is death; everything previous,
happenstance, a lavish understanding
of ourselves that no one else shares.
Her mother calling from the kitchen window,
the night sky tangled in the trees,
that's how she remembers it.

Autumn
After the hot afternoons of summer,
climbed the roof to sweep away pine needles,
clearing the gutters for the coming rains.
A chill darkened the sky,
only the bones of clouds remained.
It's autumn, not winter,

that turns men into martyrs.

The windows rattle more often.

He pauses from his chores,

pulls a pack of cigarettes from a pocket,

lights one and sucks the smoke down

the way a man gulps air when he doesn't know

how long he'll have to hold his breath.

Autumn, the season that is The Coffee Cup;

the season of men on roofs,

of crickets mourning their wounds;

autumn, the season between.

The windows rattle more often.

It won't last forever, not even the owls

that spend their nights laughing at us.

This Wasn't

I nailed a spider's shadow to the wall
putting an end to the shrill
sound of a web being spun.
Three days later I removed the nail.
The dead spider fell to the ground.
The sun was free to go on its way.
This wasn't the first time
I've regretted the hammer.

Notes from the Interview

Occasionally someone asked
to be buried with a clock.
And for a small fee we did.
A kitchen clock that once hung
on an old woman's wall
—we placed it on the chest,
folded the arms, closed the lid.

Now you know. The ticking
you heard lying with a lover
in grass behind the headstone
as you loosened each other's clothes
wasn't a want-filled heart.
Then the quiet when you held
each other's breath and forgot to exhale.

I've Tried to Explain This Before

If there's blood on my palms it's an accident.
If there are words left on the table
like picked-over chicken bones, it's an accident.
If the sand on the beach found its way,
that can be explained. Now
when it rains, I understand.
When the noise crawls into the corner
don't tell me it's over. Each day,
I swear, each day is a sacrifice.
My heart remains at home
growling in the dark.
The new promises, at the top
of a flagpole, snap in the wind.
The new poisons, and this is
the best part, the new poisons,
not all are fatal. So
drink up, I tell myself.

The Invention of Fiction

1

It took seven years to teach my dog to play checkers.
Too complicated to explain here
but the one time I lost to him
instead of feeling proud I felt terrible.
Drool slid from his tongue onto the captured pieces.
This is where I admit to being small.

2

I came upon a stone brushing its teeth,
something seldom seen; stones
are loath to show desire or skill.
We can pretend this is impossible,
pretend here the truth is absent.
But there are things people see they never admit.

3

An oak in bloom at the bottom of the sea.
Dark water flowing through its branches.
Because you've never seen it
doesn't mean it's not there.
This is why fiction was invented,
to do the dirty work of belief.

Marie Gonzalez

RICK BURSKY was born and raised in New York City.
Immediately following high school he spent four years
as a paratrooper in the army; following that with college,
earning a BFA from Art Center College of Design in
Pasadena and then an MFA from Warren Wilson College.
His first full-length collection of poems, *The Soup of
Something Missing,* was published by Bear Star Press
(2004) after winning the Dorothy Brunsman Poetry Prize.
Hollyridge Press published his chapbook, *The Invention
of Fiction.* He has twice been nominated for a Pushcart
Prize. Rick Bursky lives in Los Angeles where he works
in advertising; teaches poetry at UCLA Extension, and
occasionally copywriting at USC's Annenberg School of
Communications.